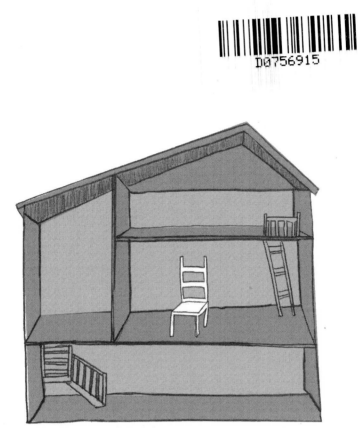

NOT A CULT

Los Angeles, CA
notacult.media

Printed in the USA

Copyright © 2018 Matthew Cuban Hernandez

No part of this book may be used or performed without written consent from the author, if living, except for critical articles or reviews.

Hernandez, Matthew Cuban

1st edition.

ISBN: 978-1-945649-17-2

Edited by Alyesha Wise, Jeremy Radin
Cover design by Cassidy Trier
Editorial design by Ian DeLucca

NOT A CULT
Los Angeles, CA

Printed in the United States of America

Cyrus!

The sky be the limit
fam! Never stop
The world needs your stories!

Contents

DUVAL

3032 is the address of the home I grew up in Jacksonville Florida. It signifies some of the best years of my life—some of the only years when my mother's health was not completely debilitating. My cousins lived one house away. David was six months younger than me and Erica was two years older. Because we lived so close to each other, my older brother and sister and I grew up feeling like we had two families.

The first section of this book is a snapshot of that time and how events, people, and places around Jacksonville shaped who I am, specifically as an educator and poet. The Paxon and Duval sections of this book encompass my time working in the juvenile justice system in Los Angeles, and how my work with incarcerated youth connects to my personal story. The neighborhood I grew up in wasn't the safest—I remember witnessing physical violence on the street directly in front of our house, ducking on the floor during home bible study due to gunshots two doors down.

The book as a whole was written during the last year of my mother's life. The gifts my mother gave me came with an unspoken obligation to continue her legacy of love. She was a true empath and medicine woman. Not long before she left this world she told me I was the first medicine man of our family. I have been focusing on claiming that title, to use my ability to make my surroundings better, to be a better teacher, partner, and man for the people in my life. 3o32 signifies all of these things. It is intimate and holds secrets that only those close to me have known prior to this book's release.

I wasn't able to finish this project before her transition, so she never got to see my name on a published book. She never got to read the words she inspired or see how much she truly molded who I am, holistically. My hope is that 3o32 can be a small piece of her that travels and spreads the medicine and love she gave the world so willingly—to my readers, to their loved ones, to my students.

3o32

My ambiguous

I am a Brown boy
embracing all that is my mix
attempting to understand my own
spill—seeking comfort within the unsteady
of my complexion, the Middle East crawling the bridge
of my nose, the Mayan reddening the fertile soil of my skin,
the rebellion in my lineage, the history of suffering and servitude
my blood survived so I could conjure this legend, the racism that could
not break the boy my father grew from, and the holy clay that molded my
mother.

gift

Because my scars
are so fresh
it makes my glow

brighter, my hugs
tighter, my care
considerate
focused on the quietest
voice, mumbling through

a song God hummed
while making dinner, snapped
"Not yet"

like testing a battery
with your heart

Her spirit
in everything
I cook

How God
held my hand,
carried a scent

like a seasoning.

a harmony

Home, built to love words
meant to calm my heart
smile wrapped in nourishment
proclaims me a king

Meant to calm my heart
my mother's voice
proclaims me a king
blood in my royalty

My mother's voice
a sweet harmony
blood in my royalty
sizzling, a quiet revolution

A sweet harmony
the child hidden laugh
revolution, a quiet sizzling
this feels like home

the child hidden in my laugh
nourishment wrapped in a smile
this feels like
home, built to love

sage advice

Around my 6th birthday I figured it out.
My parents weren't whooping me because I was bad;
they were whooping me because they liked it.

After hours of crying, this was the lesson
I found in the belt. Lessons
my immigrant parents knew too
intimately. My father flashed anger
with a furrowed brow. I think about the beating
that christened this legacy.

In first grade my cousin and I stole
candy from the teacher's desk after school.
During class, if you were well behaved
you got a little star by your name.

Somehow our names always end
starless. We were hood kids
so we took things we couldn't afford
into our own hands.

An advanced lesson in
"Normalization of a deviant".
We were caught, lights on,
pockets full of Jolly Ranchers.

Mother's stress, father's snap

For them, there was never
an easy option. Do you want the shoe
or the broomstick? The belt, the bible,
or the race car track?
How long do you need to cry
before you wash your face?
Some lessons you digest quicker.
Still, all my decisions
start with their voices
bouncing between my ears.

given in blood

Yesenia, my big sister,
the second womyn I knew.
Raised around matriarchs,
regal in small and brown.
The cut in words. The force of nature
known as mother.
My sister taught me
to write, showed me bullies
take shape anywhere—
sometimes in the ones who grade you,
judge, protect, and befriend
you. The world will determine
you're smart by what it takes
and how much you allow it.

My sister showed me trial
and error. The first born,
showing me
what is
possible through
what has been.

the homes that hold

If these walls could talk, they'd yell and creak into place
like old bones. Whisper about the bruises and laughter.

They'd say they could no longer hold all these hushed
secrets—how they swell like driftwood.
They'd say insecurities and doubt steam like boiling
water, that this home is a pressure cooker with no vent,
a bomb waiting.

These walls leak paint like sweat from skin, turn
everything into the first hour of *What Dreams May Come*.
The grinding of teeth like an ache in hinges. If these walls
could speak, they'd mirror humidity with anxiety, both
burdened when lights are off and the air is recycled,
allowing the warmest part of their frame to become
the room I choose to rest in.

When alone, the apartment sways with old memories.

Recalling breath as their favorite song. Once, I nearly
stopped playing. How helpless it must feel, to be alive
only to observe.

They remember when I was a child, tattooing their skin
with the inches I grew. When they were trees, the sky was
the walls that held them. How we all trudge to find beauty
in the sun's rising. How we don't notice until gutted to become
someone else's safe space. A place to blossom, fresh, grow
strong—until hollow.

If these walls could talk, they wouldn't.

They'd sit silent and nod as if to say, *There is nothing to say.*
Just enough strength to hold up the roof. Just enough memories
to keep the walls from caving in with eyes for windows
and scars like scuffs on the floor.

a safe space

My favorite game is
Zelda: Ocarina of Time.
I would start when I was feeling bad,
finished when I was fine.

I could tell my mom was sad.
She's in the kitchen crying,
I made promises, told her
I would fix it with my rhymes.

Hey mama. You wouldn't
let me play it, right? Not until
I got my grades up, I studied
day and night.

Finally, when the day came,
I only played it twice
spoiled, wanted newer games
but couldn't even pay the lights.

She told me keep my goals in sight,
told me keep my vision tight.
She must have seen me on that mic,
on that night I came alive-

13 years old and gave that open mic some life,
my daddy said don't
rot my brain, but I did it anyway.

I used to play *Final Fantasy*
four days. Literally.
My file filled over 190 hours.
The original PlayStation could not speak
so my summer reading was "FF7" through "FF10".
I once watched my brother beat the entirety
of *Star Fox* standing on his feet. Before
we discovered these games were the closest thing to a vacation
my family could afford, the closest thing to excitement
my neighborhood could harvest without harm.
Light or dark, good or evil.

Video games have been scientifically proven
to significantly increase creativity,
sense of courage, problem solving skills
loneliness, carpal tunnel, and social awkwardness.

It is the urge to keep playing to the next
checkpoint. The guilt
of a neglected gym membership.

The dim glow. The faint hum,
harbinger of joy.

where adolescence

When I was a younger man
all I had was my word
my focus, a door to new life
my heart, still full and waiting

All I had was my word.
Voice, suppressed
heart. still. full. waiting.
unsure I'd ever know intimate

Voice, a quiet scream.
a door of opportunity.
unsure I'd ever know intimate.
mixed boy, learning to smile

A door of opportunity
discovering appreciation starts with self
mixed boy, learning to smile
my chest, the canvas I painted on

Discovering appreciation starts with self
my focus, a door to new life
my chest, the canvas I painted on

When I was a younger man

became a monicker

If I told you I knew nothing
about my culture, would you judge, ask why
"Cuban", if I can't speak to my elders?
Would you question my heritage, call me sell
out, gringo, ask me to define gringo,
see my brown as counterfeit or
distraction? Maybe
introduce me to the ESL student
whose name I'd mispronounce, assume
I am not the music
my grandfather blossomed from,
believe there is no trumpet in my chest.
I, a chameleon blending into safety.
All the broken english
glued together. Conversations
I'll never have
with my grandparents. The roots
of a family tree I've never seen.
Embarrassment of "Yo no se" or "Un poquito."
Still I am Ivanna's skin, tangle of her hair,
the brightest flag my body can wave. Uncertainty
in everything I am, making me everything
I'll never be. Enough
to know the tropical my father
carries in his bilingual, the steam
sweating over my mother's hands
while passing heirlooms through her recipes.
My diaspora, the Yoruba sitting quiet in my blood,
pride that comes with the reclaiming of
your name
or just being a mixed boy.

foreshadowed

I'm afraid the car I wrecked
in high school will, one day, find its way
into my aches.

Most days start with joints popping,
head swimming like I woke up in a fishbowl—
like I plagiarized lines from my mother's script.

Her veins would harden
from atrophy. Her pain, the future
I'd be forced to dance with.

I'm afraid she'll never hug my children—
all she'll be is legend,
stories I'll never live up to.

Every ache I feel
for the rest of my life

a ghost of hers.

A temper

My father gave me his fuse—
a fast flammable rope
burned at both ends,

a shadow waiting silent
in my blood, clouding sight,
forcing red my complexion,
the following regret.

Once he kicked out the landlord,
told him *I'm not fresh off the boat,
I know my rights.*

Growing up
he was always right,
modeling our happiness
even when we had to move, even
when his simmer boiled
everyone's smile.

Only Olga

Breathe, baby boy.

That rumble in your chest
is no longer a heartbeat.

Remember when you were just a heartbeat, nothing

but the never-want of your father, ovaries
that birthed you bright.

Do you remember the first time the wind was knocked
out of you, left you reaching for what was no longer there?

Do you remember the first time Aunt Lourdes walked in,
told you she was no longer here? Do you remember
wanting to be there, or at least wanting to be clear?

Do you remember when David jumped out of that tree,
landed hand and knee in dog shit? That was the first time
you and George called him *Dookie Boy.*

Do you remember the first times you started to tune out?
How the only time you heard Spanish in your house
was through yells, tears and muffled novellas?
How ironic that those stories could never match the drama
of your own life. Do you remember the game of Life,
Domino's, Uno, tiny lizards caught with mouths open,
hissing, clamped down on earlobes like earrings?

Do you recall more hood than heritage, your native
language silent as your grandfather's deathbed, tears
flushed out to greet a stale hospice air,
eyes kicking and screaming, trying to hold back?

Do you remember the first time you pretended stupid
to mask your dyslexia, to maintain a constant C?
Remember, baby boy, you will only ever be faking

average. How many times did you want to silence
all this savage with havoc—tempting more lead
out of the barrel of a gun than the stalk of a pen?

Ironic to sleepwalk through a life
most people dream of living.

When is it a good time to stop living life
as a wrecking ball? Do you know how to slow
all that momentum—use it to destroy
the dilapidated parts of your self esteem
for a better you initiative?
When will you take initiative?

If God is every molecule and every molecule
is what makes us, then writing out your own
existence proves that God is in your makeup.

Your gift is an obligation to your birthright.
Do you know how lucky you are to speak
these cuts? Most people don't trust the truth.

When is it a good time to grow up,
baby boy? When is it a good time to stop
thinking like a baby

boy, that rumble in your chest
is no longer a heartbeat.

It's everything you're capable of.

Olgita y Ivanita

Your laugh more cackle than bellow.
Your smile a gate like open arms, to say
"You are all welcome."

Here, you would sing loud
and off key— never without
sweets, never angry,
the closest to holy I've ever known.

It's interesting how the spirit grows
stronger the weaker the flesh becomes.

Maybe life is an option.
Do I explode or breathe deep?

You never seemed afraid
even when the cancer came or when…

You fought for family until your daughters'
arms became strong
enough. You left my mom
early in her life. She left early in mine.

Now the angels smell
like yuca. They all sing
a little off key.

silenced

I'm scared
to ask
have you been
here before
have you
seen these
mountains
has this sun
ever set
on your skin
how much
did you
not have
so this could be
mine
I am
the king
of spoiled
today was

palms
outside
windows
the sky
burning across
the peaks
your day
insufferable
hours
on your feet
the pride
of providing
a silent prayer
for mercy
silent
as a bedroom
unbearable
a matriarch
alone

PAXON

Grew

Home taught me
to take care of
responsibilities —
even if you are left hungry,
no one to check if you ate.

From a world of never,
starved, always feeding, leftovers
as tomorrow's nourishment.

My city is an oyster.
A small bit of nothing but still full.
Treasures waiting to pry themselves
into existence. Jacksonville,
Florida. Almost, but not enough —
stifled is the language
most spoken.

Surplus of ready-to-fight,
burning everything to the ground.
My city of bridges, hugged by a river,
neighbor to an ocean.
All the holy it pretends to be,
the traps it holds, every hood
it hollows. My city
of murder and God —

then turned joy

I've been searching for joy / circumventing all pleasure / stumbling into my voice / vices switch with no effort / knowing life's not forever / tryna' keep it together / burdens heavy as ever / so I live like / whatever

I know you feel indifferent / couldn't survive this mission / the devil's finger licking / reading my boys to submissions / My path to redemption / comes from the bars that I've written / hoping God will listen / chill amongst y'all as witness / I'm washing dishes in my soul's kitchen / I stay spiritual / yet immature / with time to pack a bowl / A Gemini, back and forth / I look back on the past and ask for more / when I was just a rascal still / a mix boy raised in Jacksonville / didn't have a lot, learned to steal / when momma used to whip us still / and she could walk around all day / and didn't stay in hospitals

When leftovers were more normal / a time portal to a time sober / with more morals / we're so hollow / a soul hollers for more morsels to eat / but you can't follow when God speaks / just give a moment for your pen to compete / I'm on track to take a seat / wherever God ask me lead / immortal lessons when I take time to teach / about progression with the life that I lead / the heart that will bleed / when judgment is cast to my students and the grit that they need / to stay alive

In the streets there is no fame in diseased / struggle that would make the mightiest weak / minus a stable environment to compete / They prey on the mind of the weak / and marketing music selling nothing but schemes / I tell them it ain't what it seems / I've tried to welcome thoughts to a planet of dreams / but my soul's to the breeze / I'm hoping to leave / I'm coping with trees / I'm ashing love to all the family that leaves / after all what can I do

I'm just a mixed boy / dyslexic / caused havoc with a pen tip / mentioned by some weak boys / who started shivering from my language / I was passed out / I was anguished / I was messed up / I was God's gift / I was telling friends I'm a hard shift / I've been writing life, a manuscript / I've had to tell y'all I'm not having it / After all this world is scared of pain / and we grew up taking baths in it / We've been nice since the bassinet / It's real life, no laughing man / Don't act like it isn't happening / children lose their lives, where does the tragedy end

When young boys pulling triggers / before learning to sign their name / make raps about killing enemies / the only way to ease the pain / Don't ask what the scripture say / Jesus wasn't here today / I hear God whisper through the wind / we discuss life every day / she knows I'll find a way / been writing raps, putting rhymes away / been making bread, no time to play / knowing I have to dues to pay / instead of being another body / laid out on the news today / been writing raps / been a truth to blaze / have to speak this heat or I'll go insane

to a desert

If I were a cactus
I wouldn't be
the biggest cactus
but I would
have the sharpest spines.

No one would bother me, but I would
be lonely. Probably thirsty.
A kaleidoscope, a psychedelic-
somehow, years of sun and ice turn my blood purple.

If I were an ocean,
I wouldn't be
a red tide, just a hot pool nearly scalding,
a dried-up fist of salt
with a little cactus
in the center.

Teaching trauma

Good energy
a chant for you
to cradle all
these blessings
all this lineage
with no story to show
the knowledge of
acknowledgement
the heart calloused
and covered the smile
melting away the sky
the trauma knotting
in a classroom
a tide pulling against
a life preserver diagnosing
the spectrum in a work-
shop breathing sage
remembering even
the good days
are exhausting
and bad may leave
everything in question
my testimony
can be a roadmap
my words the clearest
truth a window opening
through concrete

for any, Challenger

Last week, two of my favorite students wrapped
their knuckles around each other. In class,
when we're aggravated or angry, we do push-ups
or listen to really cool beats. The other day, on my sign
in sheet, in the comment section usually reserved
for the principal, one of my boys wrote, "Great class."

At the Challenger Memorial Juvenile Detention Center,

a youth prison named after a space shuttle that exploded,

a failed mission- there is a dog pound at the front gates. You can hear
whining and barking as tires roll through gravel. In the yard,
you can see the lights of the state penitentiary directly behind.

Most of my boys joke and say this will be their next step.
But in my class, I show them poems —
always the powerful and always my favorite. I tell them
there is a future in words. I show them my past, the dirt
I crawl through, the voice I stumbled on — the same voice
they can find searching the right conversations.

We speak of memories, acknowledge and agree that we
are the sum of what we recall. Their growth is my process
and I love to watch them blossom. Each poem, a petal
forcing its way from a bud, a little more assured
each time. Each step, a little more confident.

I don't teach kids to write poems.

I teach them to walk in their own skin. I teach them to own
their skin when they walk. Sometimes I stand in front
of a classroom and my students look like abandoned
homes in a neighborhood the city has forgotten.

I give them notebooks, I give them tool belts and talk
them into believing anyone can be carpenters.
These words are nails and boards. These poems are houses.
Build them carefully. Someone might need to live here.

I tell them the sentences you need to focus on don't end
with a gavel, but with a period. *Let me show you
how to make them with your own hands. Your story
is important so, write it down.*

And they do. Some laugh, some cry. I say it's okay.
Our emotions are like lightning
bugs—if we keep them bottled they will die,

and a person who doesn't feel is just a photograph.

I tell them to dream, then edit.

Feel for your truth like a switch when engulfed
in all life's dark. This universe loves honesty, so don't
hold your tongue or pull your punches. You can be great.

Each poem, a petal forcing its way from a bud,
a little more assured each time. Each step, a little
more confident than the last. I tell them I love them,
because most of the time they never hear that
I tell them no matter what their P.Os have told them
no matter what the world has shown them

that they are not a failed mission, to me.

incarcerated

Rejuvenation / my affirmation / in formation / of purpose / a
workshop / turning students / into wordsmiths / brown skin /
telling my kids / their stories are bugles / to awaken / elevation
comes from turning / the losses taken / to progress / changing
fear to trust / and anger to possibility

Knowing loss

Heavy as a gun
a stack of poems'
enough lead
to make a bullet.

His name scribbled
like a tag, a manifesto
for survival.

Incarceration plays
the clock and calendar
like an uptight conductor.

We record our music
and become our favorite
song, stories about dreams,
about friends gone too
early and family missed

yet all the melodies
sound like warnings,

all the music glows
like an exit sign

an ending come
too soon.

Before 20 years
grows into a memory
before owning a car
becomes a burden
or renting an apartment
and turning it to sanctuary
before leaving his city
and letting happiness
partner guilt

I archive all the hymn
I can find, let my mind drift
to apologies.

If all these poems
about change
still allow him to slip away
have I not failed?

He, another coat to carry
another teenager gone
leaving guilt
as the sole survivor.

I neglect myself as a coward's
suicide, how the importance
of living gets tied to this
ministry of work, how every
day is a tug at the rope,
a tightening around fortitude.

Ask me why he was
locked up. Why I found him
in a camp. Ask if his grades
were good, if he was gang
affiliated, then took the bus
to his house at night,
how does one survive
without affiliation
when the cold becomes
a countdown
to your annual trigger.

Does death make change
impossible? Will hurt always
be the loudest relative
at our gatherings?
Is trauma the only gift
Los Angeles grandfathers
to its educators?

Will all my children be ghosts?

and the depression

The warm smoke I breathe
gasping for air
the reach without hold
the focus to do anything

Gasping for air
the patience that flusters
the focus to do anything
the frigid autopsy of regret

The patience that flusters
the finding after the frantic
the autopsy of frigid regret
acknowledging the hurt

The finding after the frantic
praying for strength
acknowledging the hurt
with truth I can't accept

Praying for strength
the reach without hold
with truth I can't accept
the cold smoke I breathe

Today is a sharp smile
bursting from my mask
picking food from my heart
hunger that never fills

Masking my burst
the love I try to manifest
hunger that never fills
a promise I forget to keep

The love I try to manifest
perfection I'll never find
a promise I'll forget to keep
the frustration I hide in my teeth

Perfection I'll never find
a constant search for genuine
the frustration I hide in my grin
the hope that harbors my happiness

A constant search for genuine
picking food from my heart
the harbor that hopes my happiness
today is a sharp smile

like a prayer

My world is emotion—
smiles, anger,
furrowed eyebrows, sharp
stares, looks that make you
question purpose.

Exposed. Opened.

A tear you can't
actualize, the magic
in creation. Words ignored
until bullied onto paper.

The things we tag,
ball up, or claim—
our set and charise
like a knockout. We are
the waiters, the clock
watchers.

When is lunch?
When is rec?
When do I see
my judge?
When is my early?
When do I go home?
When do I get
put on?

The other day, two boys
couldn't stop speaking
about worship—
called it "The Almighty
666," the soul, the only worth
they feel, purpose
they don't understand.

Praying to a black hole,
like pouring hope
in an abyss. Still,
another student is
fittingly named Angel
and loves hugs,
when he writes,

his smile erupts—

and hope becomes a unicorn
for a moment

Compton

If I'm being honest, I don't think I'm doing too well
and I don't think I've done much better. I keep telling
myself how important my work is, but it's hard to see
when a shift ends. A meeting this afternoon, and I feel
I'll be threatened or fired. Not sure If I care. Not sure
if it matters. My students are not my students. I am
told there is a thin line between what I do and baby-
sitting. I am struggling to oppose the thought. Fellow
educators look down their nose, question my credibility,
jab at the magic I fight to wear. Yesterday, Marvin
told me he almost died, told me the bullet that kissed
his friend's neck zipped past his own. He writes,
my lesson. We talk about violence, about childhood.
All the feelings we know,
that only know a clenched jaw. Only visualize the next
time to be the end they've been waiting for. This fear
is stifling, it tells me the honesty I trudged for is a cloud.
Tells me it's out of reach with nothing genuine to actually
hold. Yet there are still so many sad questions, too many
questions marked on tongues meant to teach. Too many
smart people scaring my students to believe in anything
other than death.

turned permanent

Jimmy killed himself last summer.
Must have been something about the L.A. heat,
the smell of rain that never comes—
turning his tag into a tombstone,
becoming the center of attention.
It would be impressive if it didn't
feel so familiar. If the thought didn't
water my palms.

When I give into my spill.

my final act
a permanent gasp
carrying a mask
everyone saw as a smile.

It may hurt at first.
Ten seconds becomes impossible,
so I understand the exhale
and the relief that comes
with letting go.

Hold your breath,
count to 44,193.

DUVAL

pleaded

God it feels like I'm falling apart at the seams / And all this pain I'm living with ain't as hard as it seems / But I keep pushing / I know it's up to me / Got herb and my inhaler, harder to breathe / Happiness, depression always tied to a breeze / Finally settled down, then decided to leave / I'm getting mad at my mirror, hating all that I see / But there's a hell inside my chest that I'm hoping to free / Find the door to my success, make it open for me / I got the blood of a soldier / Check my family tree / Respect to everyone / How a man's meant to be / I'm in the future, the past, where insanity leads / I'm feeding fuel to enemies like bringing sand to a beach / Giving English to elders understanding my speech / I know there's a place warm and waiting for me / Trigger finger to my head / hoping heaven I'll see

to stay

1.
To spend some time in a place, in a situation, with a person or group.

> *In 2012 I toured for 35 days through the midwest and east coast with a musical genius. Secretly I just wanted a good excuse to get drunk and hear him play every night. It became an internship in the art of da hustle. With my survival dependent on the performance I would give.*

2.
Remain in a specified state or position.

> *During the day, if workshops or driving did not take precedent, I'd sleep. Sometimes for the entire day. Something about the access to free wifi, free time, and a room with a locked door allowed me to remain in a state of unconsciousness for hours.*

3.
To hold out or endure, as in, a contest or task.

> *During long nights, in between the high of a great show and the 600 miles until the next, my mind would drift. The headlights becoming blurred images dancing through the rearview. The road melting into a dark tunnel. A private journey, a test, with loneliness and death resting on my eyelids, snoring louder with every   slow   blink…*

4.
To keep up, as, with a competitor.

> *I would open our sets. We did "rock, paper, scissors" on our first show and, lucky me, it stuck for all 40 shows, but I loved it. My tourmate told me a lot of performers would have a hard time keeping up with him. We were partners, but feeding from the same trough; healthy competition. Still, every night was a feast.*

5.
Poker term: to continue in a hand by matching a bet or raise.

> *Once, while touring in Cleveland, I let a poet friend take my car to our next show in DC while I stayed in pursuit of "booty." My tourmate at the time begged me to reconsider, told me he was not coming back, I'd need to find my own way to the next gig. I made the choice to stay. Then, only moments after, I bumped into a painting on "booty's" wall. It fell shattered on the floor, irreparable. Jokingly I said, "I hope that wasn't important." Her eyes watered, then burst into flame. "That was my grandmother's, she gave me that before she died... last month"*

6.
To stop or halt.

> *Your inner voice often has really good ideas, you only have to be smart enough to listen.*
> *All the signs laid themselves at my feet and laughed through the weekend.*

7.
To pause or wait, as for a moment before proceeding or continuing; linger or tarry.

Nashville, Tennessee, at BB King's Blues Bar. Packed house, all the product sold and a line waiting for my laptop to burn CDs! Only one thing can make this night better, weed! After the show, I begin the search. The most disheveled person could likely point me in the right direction, and upon finding him I ask, "

ME: Hey bro, you ahh... know where ahh... A person might be ahh... able to come up on some weeeeeed?

HIM: I ain't got no weed! All I got is this Crack!"

ME: Well ya know, crack really isn't what I was looking for, persay—

HIM: Hey man! Crack ain't no worse than weed!

ME: Bro it's fucking crack!

HIM: Hold up man and watch my back while I hit this shit.

He hits the shit, I watch his back.

HIM: Hey man, do you want to smoke this crack?

For a moment I thought, No one's ever actually offered me crack. Do I really want to try some crack??

8.

Archaic. to cease or desist.

"Shotgun"—A poem I'd recently found strength in. Something about screaming my suicide note to strangers across the country. Something about finding strength in reliving my weakest moment every night. I'd close my set with "Shotgun." During my set the audience and I would laugh and forget the world for a moment. But at some point I needed to tell someone to stay. Even if the person was me. Giving 100 percent to an empty bar, to prove to the world I'm still alive in spit. And the music would bring me back every night. No matter how much I poured myself out, my partner played his set and restarted my chest. For 20 minutes, I got to be a rock star—or at least a shitty back up singer on all his songs. With the alcohol dancing in my bones and the depression rattling all my hinges, every show empty or sold out, felt like we were the coolest guys in the room. I tried to tell myself it's easy to leave. To grab a handful of your last and stop your story in a grave. It would've been too easy to let my brother's shotgun be the last thing to kiss my cheek. But to stay? To stay is to continue, endless tokens in a game impossible to beat from a hole. Still, I'm not sure if fear keeps me. With my own shadows blocking all the exits. All the reasons to stay, staring back at me in every reflection.

awake

The woman who said *yes*
to forever believes
in every ounce of me.

Somehow my depression
yells louder. Somehow
doubt stands at the top

of my resume, turning out
the lights and locking
all the doors, telling me

to wrap myself in fuck it
and sleep for the next
600 hours. I've got this

eject button that sends me
back to my mother's arms,
will let me help my father

get rest and put a dam
on the trauma I'll carry
if I let my mother die

Now that option is gone
and guilt's bent its knee
for regret. At least

they'll have each
other. At least
they won't be alone.

on the inside

I know
My chest is a holding cell.
Emotions wait
for bail or sentencing.

There is just as much beauty
as ugly. Most won't find it.
Most don't look.

I know
My smile is powerful.
All my love
generates from it.

Love is one of the most
important gifts I often
forget to give myself.

I know
Teaching in juvenile detention
camps, all this youth, these stories
heavy as guilt, heavy as burdened
family, heavy as the crosses
tattooed on the faces of students.

The importance of words
like pieces on a chessboard,
knowing the moves
but blind to strategy.

When I leave this life,
when I take in air for the last time,
I will be remembered by what
I didn't say, remembered
by every student
I failed, by their laughter
after they slip
through my fingers.

When I am alone, I am not alone.
I am accompanied by anxiety
and depression, the wardens
of my happiness.

When I say this out loud it hurts
those who love me.

I am loved.

My apartment fills with people
I manifest, the strings
still holding me together.

This world makes me
angry. Things that should
make clear sense do not.

I am afraid for my children and wife.

Violence is not always an answer
as much as it is a necessity

Love is not always an answer
as much as it is a necessity

I don't know what will change
without both.

to embrace

She is a stockpile
of information, stories
waiting to curl, then
expand
in the mouth—a smile
crawling across my skin.

She sits, head nodding
to a melody
I may have heard, but never
called home.
She nods, typing, soft,
invisible.

The Tea Drinker.

She, the edit
I miss, an energy
my body would collapse
over. The "right now"
she holds
for every moment, the voice
she keeps
in her throat, a bullet,
chambered
as she types.

Laptop a road
to perdition, manuscript
a holy scripture, a movement
even when still.
Grace, even
in her awkward.

She is the God I know
answering prayers
for the God
that blessed me
with her.

my mother

When all my memories become my pain I'll fly away. I only wear this mask of strength so I don't cry today. I know I've tried to stay, depression lies to me. But all this temperature in my blood is where my fire stays. Mama are you listening? I'm speaking through my dreams. It's hard to hear my blessing when surrounded by my screams. It's hard to count my blessings when they only come from sneeze. I'm asking for forgiveness while I'm beggin on my knees. I'm trying to gather energy to find the urge to care, but happiness was absent when I stepped in urgent care. Mama are you listening I'm asking if you're there. You were sick and tired all my life I don't see how that's fair. God, tell me what's your purpose, why you sent my angel home. Every day I see her in the mirror like a clone. I'm crying for my Daddy, he don't need to be alone so I'm searching for the words to try and save him through my poems.

My mind always drifts away when trying to focus. I call my mama's phone when I'm alone and feeling hopeless. Of course she doesn't answer, doesn't even have a voicemail. Deep breaths in my reality and I am in hell. My pen's still, my stencil. Be whatever heaven tells me that I must instill, this isn't real, I can't feel, how the fuck my mama leave this world from taking doctors' pills? I got my fill of every lie the hospital would tell me. You can take my happiness to keep my mama healthy. This system failed me when they let my mama slip away. If doctors really cared my mom would still be here today. This anger channels though my poems never goes away. Leave me broken, bloody, please just let my mama stay.

What's your purpose, God? Tell me what you're training me for?
I feel so worthless God I don't think I can take anymore. You
burned me straight to the core, with no escape from the storm.
Now I'm drowning evil surrounds me saying *"pray to me more"*.
My mama's teaching could reach me even if earth she was leav-
ing, demons deceive me, come when my spirit is weak and I'm
grieving. I used to believe that all this happened for reasons but
that would change with the seasons, and taking you was some
treason when all we pray to was Jesus and all he gave you was
weakness. My hopes were depleted. Gave me the Bible to read it
but your survival was needed. I bet your view now is cynic, the
tops of mountains you reached so God we'll never be even, only
through dreams mama's speaking. So God just tell me your rea-
sons. God Just tell me your reasons. God just tell me.

to manifest

I won't allow the safe bet
to content and stifle.

A bullet bouncing
in my mouth, ivory
curtain of teeth.

This body, a rusty ship, or
a bottle ready to be broken
against as a christening.

The journey my decisions
anchor me to, everything
that will and the doubt
that will not.

what is built for me

I think of my home,
the comfort I worked
to shape. The family I hope to
raise, children I will one day watch
grow. Here is where my fear takes root.
I imagine the hinges buckle. The locks snapped
and my front door trampled. Someone unwanted, uninvited.

Turning sanctuary to welcome mat. I visualize myself
pushing my family to the back. Here is where
a gun might perhaps present itself. Would it
even matter? I think of an elementary
school. My son and his class-
mates, a gluttony
of possible
so bright
the darkest
crave to snuff out.
Where do all my feelings
for gun control go then, when
choosing a side can get me killed?
All the numbers the world can make,
telling me why or why not. Still, if the zombie
apocalypse was today everyone of us would be running
to the nearest pawn shop. It's terrifying and irrational,
fighting fire with a hand grenade. I'm afraid
of getting shot, so I buy a gun and
increase my chances of getting
shot. I guess I just wonder
where this all started.
Like who noticed
they were
bigger

and stronger
and decided to take
advantage. Night is a flood
of worry, thinking of what some big man
might do to destroy my home. I want to change my reaction,
put my body on the line with a thousand other people and wrap
ourselves around City Hall or the mayor's house and refuse
to move, refuse to move until we follow so well, casing for
something to answer our late night fears and calm
our paranoia. Somewhere in all of our minds
none of us truly feel "ready." Change
will not happen peacefully, and it
rattles me to say that. After all,
change is the only thing
that's guaranteed.

The smile she turned into

How could I have called it love
before now? Yesterday

I saw you for the first time, fresh
eyes to a canvas I've painted for years.

Were all my smiles counterfeit?
All throwaway poems? Rooms where

I studied my craft but never felt at one with?
Did I understand content or only calm

between a tidal push? How could it
have not been so clear? So easy you fit.

How could I fight against your current?
You, the only warmth I don't second-guess.

I've seen self-conscious in your blush—
blind to all the gorgeous in your everything.

I hear my mother's wisdom when you speak.
Your patience for the youth we love,

the hurt we partner when they disappear.
The blade of your tongue, ready

for slit. I prayed for you before I knew
the sass in your dimples. And when our heat

finally pooled, I was still a Florida Boy
fresh from oppression, visiting a city you

owned like you grew it in your garden.
Your smile told me I did well

as you traveled trains that swam through
your town like arteries. Sometimes

the future stares us in the face.
Sometimes, she wears a headwrap

and escaped a city she wanted out of.
And isn't that ironic? So like love—

found us a mess, turned us beautiful.

a perfect day

This morning, I slept in.
My bed had never been so warm.
My pillow, never so inviting.
No alarm clock waiting to ring
or engagement to meet-
guilt free sleep.

Feet to floor, eyes adjusting
to the most magnificently rolled blunt,
which burned every drag as if it were the last,
at a temperature even the sativa preferred.

My shower, my grooming,
feeling as if I'd never been as clean.
The water, a perfect warmth
like a million tiny hugs
welcoming me to a good day.

I noticed the smell first—
cinnamon and soft, salivating and sizzling,
brought my taste buds to tears.

A meal suitable enough to be my last—
a mouth orgy,
foodgasm
'til food baby
greatest meal of my life

Voices of representatives pulling me
away telling me all overdraft fees

have been returned
just because i'm awesome?!
Said my account wasn't much
but my personality was rich.

Line clicking over to my mother

Telling me the lupus is gone.

The diabetes walked out the door
and took all the terminal with it.

Said she laid in the Sun for hours
just to feel God's kiss on her cheek.

Said my brother is master chief at JFD
and Jessica is running for mayor.
David is a successful entrepreneur
and Erica's teaching at Yale.
Lourdes and Charlie travel the world,
have never been so healthy.
And that my father is the man he is
and the best hand God could have dealt me.

Then I got booked
O'Brien
Kimmel
Fallon
Colbert
The Daily Show and
Fresh Air which is exactly
what I needed

I proceeded
to take a bike ride up a mountain hill
but it's easy as going down
my muscles pulling
every inch towards a more stellar view.
At peak the sun Picassos the sky.

My pen and pad
precise and sharp
felt familiar and new all at once
with my next five books written
in one afternoon.

My friends took me to a concert
rockin bells, seats close enough to be pulled
on stage by Prince to sing Purple Rain
and it's such a shame
our friendship had to end.

I freestyled with my heroes and killed it
until I was asked to go on tour
but I told Kendrick
I had to check my schedule

Went home to the woman of my dreams
made love only rivaled by the food
we ate.

We held each other
like we invented it.

For:

Ivanna, Jorge Sr., Yesenia, Jorge Jr., Lourdes, Charlie, Erika, David, Morgan, Alyesha, my students, Duval County, for the sadness and all the joy of overcoming

About the Author

Matthew 'Cuban' Hernandez is a poet, speaker, and performance coach from Jacksonville, Florida. He has toured as far as Abu Dhabi and nearly every major city in the United States and Europe, performing, teaching and coaching poetry. A teaching artist for nearly ten years, Matthew has spent the last four years working in youth detention centers across Los Angeles County. He has opened for artists such as Wu-Tang and performed for platforms such as BuzzFeed and NPR. Matthew is also a three time Southern Fried poetry slam champion and an award-winning poetry coach. Cuban's favorite activity is making people feel great; sometimes he does this through poetry.